D0480250

OR 6.1.94

Victorian and Edwardian
BRIGHTON
from old photographs

1 Children in Queens Park, *c.* 1900. One can only wonder what was in the bottle

2 (*overleaf*) Kings Road; the lower esplanade, the enclosures and Brunswick Lawns, in 1891. Brunswick Terrace, designed by Amon Wilds and Charles Augustus Busby, was built between 1824 and 1830. The enclosures were replaced by the present gardens in 1925–1926

Victorian and Edwardian

from old photographs

JOHN BETJEMAN

and

J. S. GRAY

Published by
B. T. BATSFORD LTD
LONDON

B. T. Batsford Ltd
4 Fitzhardinge St, London W.1
Printed and bound in Great Britain by
Jarrold & Sons Limited, Norwich, Norfolk
First published in 1972
7134 0119 2

CONTENTS

3 A chair mender at work, 19 September 1890. He was sitting in Portland Road at the junction with Sackville Road

ACKNOWLEDGMENTS

The authors are most grateful to the libraries, companies, institutions and individuals through whose kindness the photographs in this book were made available. In particular they wish to thank, for the pictures indicated:

Earl Baldwin of Bewdley for illustration 111; Brighton College: 90, 91, 92; Brighton Polytechnic: 78; The Librarian, Brighton Public Library: 15, 23, 27, 34, 52, 60, 89, 109, 116, 120, 129, 131, 133, 136, 147; British Railways, Southern Region: 82, 135; The Misses Brown: 106; C. H. Cuttress: 119; Field & Cox Limited: 81; F. Frith & Co. Ltd: 13, 36, 110, 139; F. W. Gregory: 117; G. P. A. Limited: 9; The Librarian, Hove Public Library: 49, 79, 98, 100, 101, 102, 103, 122; Lancing College: 154; The Museum of British Transport: 142; The Publishers: 108; Radio Times Hulton Picture Library: 12, 61; Reeves Collection, *Sunday Times:* 124; Roedean School: 125; Aubrey Ruff: 1, 14, 30, 31, 33, 50, 112; Religious Society of Friends: 5; St Aubyn's Magazine: 134; R. Stent: 148; Sussex County Cricket Club: 126; E. F. Thomas: 107, 137; Valentine and Sons Limited: 2, 28, 44, 48, 95, 152.

The remainder of the photographs are from the collection of Mr J. S. Gray.

INTRODUCTION

Few places gave so much pleasure as Brighton. 'Farewell Old Ocean's Bauble, glittering Brighton!' wrote the brother poets, Horace and James Smith in 1813. *Brighton, Old Ocean's Bauble* is the title Professor E. W. Gilbert gave to his informative, poetical and brilliant book published in 1953. This was the first authoritative work on the English seaside industry as a whole and viewed historically and aesthetically.

When I first remember Brighton in 1918 and stayed with my parents at The Old Ship Hotel, we searched in the town for the Sussex of flint cottages with hipped roofs, and tea shops with warming pans, among the lanes, and of course we went out to Rottingdean to admire the house of Burne-Jones (fig. 108). Kemp Town then was regarded as seedy, and Hove as more aristocratic. Brighton and Hove were still a resort rather than flats for commuters to London. Stucco was regarded as false and the *Little Guide to Sussex* (1900) described the now rightly admired Pavilion as 'architecturally contemptible'. I can remember the look of amazement on the faces of antique dealers and print sellers in the lanes of Brighton, when I asked whether they had any engravings of George IV. To them he was a drunken profligate, a liar and as false as the stucco which covered the buildings associated with him. They had no engravings of him, and I had to buy one in London.

In 1935 Osbert Sitwell and Margaret Barton wrote their social history of Brighton (1770–1830) called *Brighton* and this was, I think, the first work to speak appreciatively of the stucco architecture of Hove, Kemp Town, and Brighton generally. In 1939 John Piper published his beautiful aquatints of Hove and Brighton, and these included views not only of the Regency and early Victorian stucco, but also of the piers, bandstands and of the Metropole before its head was

4 The West Pier from the beach, about 1868. The first pile was sunk in March 1864, and the pier was opened on 6 October 1866

5 Friends Meeting House, Ship Street, 1875. The Religious Society of Friends erected this building in 1805 when they moved from North Street; it was enlarged and extended in 1876. Prominent Brightonians, members of the Society, seen here include Marriage Wallis and Daniel Hack

cut off. Since then Antony Dale has written the *History and Architecture of Brighton* (1950) and Clifford Musgrave his work on the Pavilion and on the furniture of the Regency period. To these last two authors and to the increasing number of writers and artists who have come to Brighton, and above all to Brightonians themselves, we owe the preservation of what is left of these glorious twin towns. Antony Dale and Clifford Musgrave helped to found The Regency Society of Brighton and Hove in 1945. It is now registered with the Civic Trust.

As this century proceeds, the architecture of the late Victorian and Edwardian ages in Brighton comes into perspective, and we can pick the good from the bad. No one will want to see destroyed the magnificent churches of Father Wagner which stood for what used to be called the 'London Brighton and South Coast religion', i.e. beautiful ceremony, singing and furnishings. No one will want to lose the West Pier (1866) now threatened, nor the Palace Pier, both of which alleviate the flat

6   Preston Circus, *c.* 1880. Longhursts' Amber Ale Brewery occupied the large site between Stanley Road (left, beyond horse and cart) and Viaduct Road (extreme right). The man is standing in the centre of Beaconsfield Road; on the left is the Stanford Arms Inn, built in 1874

prospect of the English Channel when days are calm, and supply gusty pleasure without the disadvantages of seasickness, when waves are high and the shingle rattles as it tumbles back on itself and waits for the next onslaught. Then how welcome too are the surviving lanes and alleyways of the ancient fishing town of Brighton which existed long before George IV rediscovered it. Still less can we spare the Squares and Crescents and human scale houses that drop down behind Kemp Town and spread inland from the flatness of Hove.

In the seventeenth century there was a conflict between the landsmen of Brighton who lived on the hill-slopes below the old parish church and the fishermen who were down by the pool. This battle was forgotten in the glorious days of royal patronage under George IV. In Queen Victoria's reign, Brighton became both a health resort and London-by-the-sea, but it was a place where you stayed in lodgings or sent your children to stay in lodgings, while you remained in London or went shooting and fishing. All the time the seaside people who kept the lodging houses and shops were the real people of Brighton and Hove. It had not yet become a commuting place. All the time too, there was a large residential population.

One of these residents was Mr J. S. Gray, who like thousands of others, has adopted Brighton. I give you, in his own words, the account of how he came here and made this collection of photographs. 'I was born at St Helens, Lancashire, but was brought to London by my parents when I was a few months old. We lived in various places, Chelsea, Lambeth and Croydon before settling in Beckenham in 1912. I was educated at Beckenham County School (1916–1920), now known as Beckenham and Penge Grammar School. In 1922 my father died quite suddenly and after a few months my mother and I moved down to Brighton, to join friends. I was then 18 years old. I still travelled daily to London on the 7.10 a.m. train but in evenings and at week-ends walked miles through the streets of Brighton and Hove, exploring the many courts, alleys and twittens, now, alas, nearly all "improved" out of existence. I memorised street names, noticed similarities of buildings in different areas and by research found the names of the builders and the periods of building. I bought all books and old Directories of Brighton, which added to my knowledge of the history and growth of the town. In 1950 I started my photographic collection with 6 old photos of Western Road, *circa* 1910, and over the years have built this up to between 4000 and 5000.'

Of all the books in this series, this one I think, has the most beautiful illustrations. They include Sussex villages on the outskirts and lanes in the old seaport, and above all people and navigation by sea and land. I look at them and wonder if Brighton wasn't more enjoyable as London-by-the-sea, tolerated by Sussex, than as the place it is only too likely to be, the realisation of the Marina-minded enemy's dream of another Costa del Sol or Benidorm. Will tall cheaply-built slabs replace everything you see in these pages?

JOHN BETJEMAN

7   The extreme eastern end of Western Road, looking west, 1902. None of these buildings now remains. Those on the right were removed in 1934 for road widening; the Churchill Square redevelopment swept away all buildings on the left as far as Clarence Street. Many of these had been built in the back gardens of houses in Grenville Place

8 'Ring-a-roses' on the Western Lawns, 4 August 1892. This is now the site of the bowling greens. The three large houses, then only recently built, were known as 1–3 Westbourne Terrace, but are now part of Kingsway

WEST BRIGHTON

9   A Punch and Judy show on the lower esplanade, west of the West Pier, 1884

10 Kings Road and the Promenade in the summer of 1864, before the West Pier was built. From west of Regency Square it looks to the distant Chain Pier. At the sea side of the Promenade there was no fence; grassy slopes intersected by small flights of steps descended to the beach below

11 (*opposite above*) West Pier. Listening to the Band playing on the open deck at the head of the pier, about 1870

12 (*opposite below*) Edwardian fashions on the Front, *c.* 1903. The Bedford Hotel (1829–1964), by Thomas Cooper, and the tall building with the iron balconies, the New Club (1876–1937) have since been rebuilt

13   Looking west over the beach from the West Pier, *c*. 1890. The Bandstand, with its adjoining enclosures, was built in 1884. The present boating pool which covers the site to the right foreground was opened on 15 August 1925

14   (*left*) Professor Reddish 'flying the foam' from the West Pier, 17 June 1904. A professional swimmer and 'water artiste', one of his feats was to dive from the pier on a bicycle

15 Goat boys and flower seller at the Brighton–Hove boundary, in the 1890's. The Hove front was then still gas lit

16 Entertainers on the beach *c.* 1870. The location is about opposite Preston Street. At this period the beach came right up to the Esplanade wall

CENTRAL BRIGHTON

17 The Brighton François–Premier style: No. 67 Kings Road, at the turn into West Street, *c.* 1870. At the right was the old George Inn, rebuilt in 1892; between was narrow Kent Street consisting of a few old houses and named after Thomas Kent the builder. None of these buildings now remains

18 (*opposite above*) The West Battery, Kings Road, about 1850. The muzzle-loaded cannon were installed in 1793, the weight of each shot being 40½ lbs. They were never fired in anger, but when fired for other reasons they generally damaged nearby windows. In the crescent behind the Battery was later built the Grand Hotel

19 (*opposite below*) The removal of the West Battery in order to widen Kings Road: lowering the flagstaff on 27 January 1858. The crescent behind the Battery (now occupied by the Grand Hotel) was called Artillery Place, and housed the Royal Navy Lieutenant in charge. The corner of Cannon Place can clearly be seen

20 (*above*) The Grand Hotel, Kings Road and the Chain Pier, November 1883. The Hotel, built to the plans of J. H. Whichcord, was opened on 23 July 1864. The still narrow south pavement was widened by some 25 feet in 1886 by being built out over arches

21 (*overleaf*) Hog boats on Brighton beach, opposite Black Lion Street about 1870. A particular feature of these 'Hoggies' was that the ratio of length to breadth was only about 2 to 1. They gradually declined in number until by 1886 only three were left. It is said that the last one was burnt in a fifth of November bonfire on the beach

22 Fishermen working on nets on the beach between Black Lion Street and Market Street, *c.* 1868. The black huts were for the storage of nets and fishing tackle. Often half an upturned boat (like the one just visible on the right) was used for this purpose

23 Fishing boats and fishermen on the beach, 1871

24   The fishing fleet on the beach just to the west of the Fish Market, about 1880. When the
Promenade was widened in 1886 the old oak fence was replaced by the present one of cast iron, with
a wooden top rail

25   Looking east from the West Pier across the open beach as far as the Chain Pier, *c.* 1870. No groynes are visible

26   Kings Road looking west and showing the West Pier under construction, in 1865. The flagpole marks the site of the West Battery, removed in 1858

27　The beach looking east towards Black Rock, *c.* 1875. The Palace Pier had yet to be built but the recently erected Aquarium (1872–1927) can be seen, and also the Chain Pier (1823–1896)

28 Bathing from machines, 1891. It is perhaps surprising that at this period men were permitted to wear just short bathing trunks. Mixed bathing from machines was first sanctioned by Brighton Council in 1899

29 Ladies surf bathing from machines, 1888. The charge for sitting on the wooden seats was one penny per person

30 'Happyjackers' on the lower promenade, c. 1900. A babel of voices urged the public to throw down pennies from the upper Promenade. From time to time they would be chased away by 'coppers'

31 This one did not run fast enough to escape. These two photographs were taken by George Ruff junior whose son, Aubrey Ruff, explains that although not taken on the same day they make an obvious pair. He also says that a punishment much favoured by the Police was to detain the boy at the Station long enough to ensure that when he did get home he would likely get a thrashing from his father for being late

32 The lower promenade in gas-lamp days, *c.* 1890. The boys seem to be playing something resembling 'Pitch and Toss'; beyond, a marbles enthusiast carefully measures his distance

33 A picnic on the groyne next to the Palace Pier, *c.* 1900. The Aquarium promenade groyne, as it was called, was built in 1876 and doubled in width in 1896

34 (*left*) A summer scene on the beach and sands, *c.* 1900

35 (*above*) Acrobatics and a barrel organ on the lower promenade, about 1900

36 (*opposite above*) The beach opposite Russell Street, 1898. In the distance is the Marine Palace and Pier, then nearing completion. At Bolla and Biucchi's Restaurant a good lunch could be had for a shilling.

37 (*opposite below*) Looking east along the beach at the foot of West Street during the summer of 1893. Following the 1886 widening of the Promenade the round shelter hall at beach level had been opened in August 1887. The transition from gas lamps to electric light standards was taking place

38 (*above*) The Marine Palace and Pier (Palace Pier) about 1900. The first pile of the Pier was sunk on 7 November 1891, and work continued until the skeleton of steelwork reached just short of the pier head. Difficulties then arose and all work ceased for some years. The Pier was opened to the public in 1899 and at the time of this photograph the theatre was being built

39 (*overleaf*) Looking north along the Palace Pier, *c* 1905, showing the Bandstand and the entrance to the Bathing Rooms

MARINE PARADE
AND EASTERN BEACHES

40 (*left*)   Marine Parade, 1871. The stretch from Eastern Street to Eaton Place was then known as Belgrave Terrace. The kerbside iron railings at one time went along the full length of the Brighton Seafront, from the Hove boundary to Kemp Town

41 (*below*) A little over a century ago there was only the beach between the sea and the Marine Parade retaining wall, built by William Lambert. Huge banks of chalk and earth were built up against the base of this wall to protect it from damage by the sea, as can be seen in this photograph from the Chain Pier, looking east, in 1869. The marine frontage is little changed to-day

42 The Aquarium, Marine Parade, and Madeira Drive, in the 1890's. The Aquarium (1872), was removed in 1927 and the reconstructed present building was opened by Prince George on 12 June 1929

43 Looking west from Marine Parade to the West Pier, about 1889, showing old wooden groynes and the chains of the Chain Pier crossing Madeira Drive to their anchorage beneath Marine Parade

44 (*opposite above*) The beach and Chain Pier from the west, 1891. The Pier had five more years of life; by October 1896, it was considered to be unsafe and was closed to the public on 9 October. During the night of 4 December it was destroyed in a severe wind and rain storm

45 (*opposite below*) The Chain Pier, Marine Parade and Madeira Drive, 1890. The pier was planned by Captain, later Sir Samuel Brown and erected under his supervision. The opening ceremony took place on 25 November 1823

46 (*above*) View from the head of the Chain Pier looking through the arched towers to the Esplanade and Marine Parade, c. 1870. At the base of the towers were shops for the sale of refreshments and knick-knacks. Apart from the head, the Pier was only 13 feet wide

47 (*opposite above*) Volk's Electric Railway: the opening ceremony, Saturday 4 August 1883. On the rear platform, Magnus Volk, the inventor; at the front, the Mayor, Alderman A. H. Cox. When first opened the line ran only from the Aquarium to the Chain Pier

48 (*opposite below*) Madeira Drive, 1891, showing the sea-wall constructed in 1870, the blocks of stone being those of the first Blackfriars Bridge, London (demolished in 1863). Volk's Railway car was descending the 1 in 28 gradient to take the line under the Chain Pier

49 (*above*) Volk's Railway car emerging from under the Chain Pier and climbing the 1 in 14 gradient to regain the level. The chains of the pier can be seen passing on either side of the verandah over Snelling's Bazaar. Above, the squat building housed the Camera Obscura

50 Building sand castles on one of the eastern beaches, *c.* 1900. In the background, Madeira Terrace can just be seen. It was built in two stages between 1890 and 1897

THE OLD TOWN

51   Boyces Street, looking through to Middle Street, about 1874. The old flint cottages were removed in 1875 when Middle Street School was reconstructed and extended. A tree can still be found in this same corner of the School playground

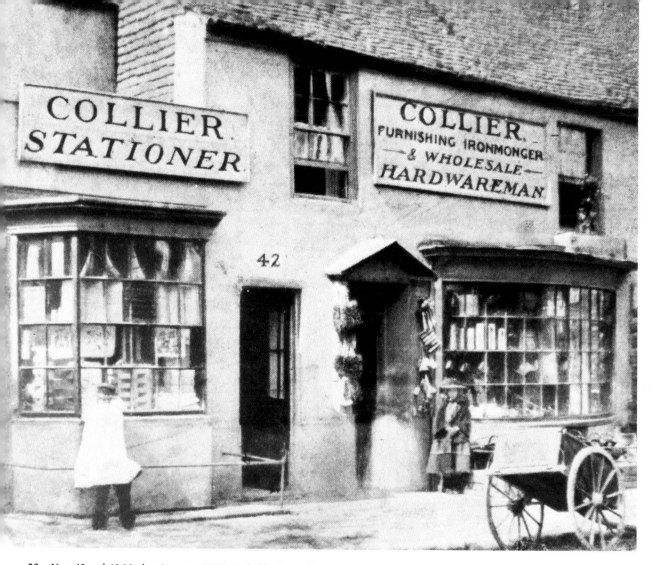

52 Nos. 42 and 43 Market Street, *c.* 1850. Probably the earliest existing photograph of a Brighton shopfront. Mrs Elizabeth Collier combined the businesses of Ironmonger and Stationer. Although these shops were demolished many years ago a Stationers business has continued on this site throughout the 120 years which have since elapsed

53 West Street, 1865. The house covered by the hoarding was 78 West Street, bought in 1767 by Henry Thrale. Among visitors to this house were Dr Samuel Johnson and Fanny Burney, who described it as 'being at the court end of the town'. It was demolished in 1866, and replaced by the Grand Concert Hall. Many changes have taken place since, but one of the seven posts still stands outside the present building

54 Pool Valley, West side, from Grand Junction Road, *c.* 1854. The old Baths were built in 1769 by Dr Awsiter and were removed a century later, in 1869, when the roadway of Pool Valley was raised to its present level. Before that, Grand Junction Road, built in 1829, was at a much higher level than the Valley, as can be seen in this photograph

55 Duke Street and Middle Street, 1868. After the widening of Duke Street in the previous year, tall trees previously between the houses were left in the roadway and are here seen being removed. Brighton's oldest school, Middle Street, is at the extreme left

56 Duke Street, looking west from the junction with Ship Street, *c.* 1850. Duke Street was then only 17 feet wide and houses on the north side hemmed in Trinity Chapel (built in 1817 by Amon Wilds for Thomas Read Kemp, as a Dissenting Chapel). All these houses were removed for street widening in 1867

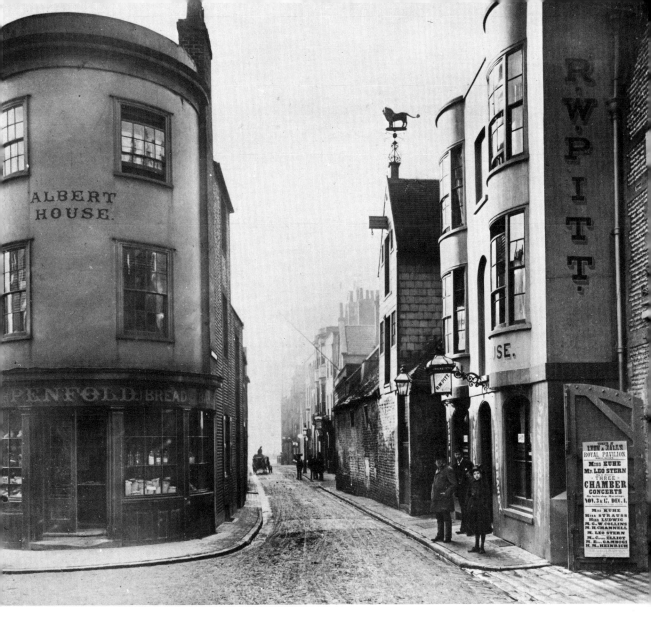

57 Black Lion Street, looking down to the sea, November 1883. A narrow street, in places only 14 feet wide, it was widened in 1889 by the removal of Albert House and the flint cottages beyond. The lintel of one of these cottages bore the date 1669

58 (*overleaf*) Looking up West Street, from the corner of South Street, *c.* 1879. The low building beyond the ladder was the Kings Head Inn. From an earlier Inn on this site, The George, Charles II, according to tradition, made his escape to France on 15 October 1651. West Street was extensively widened in the 1930's and all buildings on the West side, except for St Paul's Church, have been demolished

59 The east front of the Town Hall in Bartholomews, about 1896. Built in 1830 to the plans of
Thomas Cooper, it was reconstructed and enlarged during the late 1890's. For some years the area
around was used as a vegetable market, while the Police Fire appliance was in a handy position

NORTH STREET AREA

60 Old houses and shops, 41–43 North Street, on the south side just above
Ship Street. The year is 1862 and second-hand booksellers are on either side
of a draper and hosier. The buildings were about to be demolished (see adver-
tisements). When this was done W. J. Smith took over all three premises and
continued trading here until 1912. Wenlock House now stands on this site

61 The Dome and Pavilion Grounds in 1866. The policeman on the left was wearing the uniform of a frock coat and top hat, but helmets were introduced a year or two later. The Dome, by William Porden (previously the Royal Stables) was converted to an Assembly Room in 1867

62 The corner of North Street and Pavilion Buildings, *c.* 1860, showing the South Entrance gates to the Royal Pavilion. These were built soon after Brighton Town Commissioners bought the Pavilion Estate in 1850. On the left corner, where the Bank is to-day, was Folthorp's Royal Library and Reading Room

63 Old houses in North Street adjoining the Chapel Royal (1793–1795), between New Road and Princes Place, in August 1875. At this point North Street was about 17 feet wide. In 1879 these buildings were demolished, leaving exposed the bare south façade of the Chapel. The entire frontage was then rebuilt in red brick, the clock turret added and the Colonnade, which at one time ran around the whole of Princes Place, was removed

64 The Unicorn Inn, North Street, January 1892. One of Brighton's famous Inns, The Unicorn was originally a farm house; the eastern portion adjoining Windsor Street was a much later addition. The projecting cant windows were very popular with customers, who could sit looking up and down the street. During the demolition of the Inn, in 1892, workmen uncovered the old Town Well, 110 feet deep, known to have been there in the time of Queen Elizabeth

65 (*left*) North Street at the junction with West Street. The photograph was taken by Edward Fox about 1875. The rounded corner building was removed in 1925, the first stage in the widening of West Street.

66 (*centre*) North Street and New Road, showing almost the full length of the Royal Colonnade which extended from No. 157 North Street to the Theatre Royal. The Colonnade, built by Cooper and Lynn, was formed in 1823; the last portion of it in North Street was removed in 1929, and only the small area in New Road now remains

67 (*below*) The grocery and provision stores of Goodwin, Foster and Brown, in 1903. This shop was on the north side of North Street at the east corner of King Street.

CENTRAL VALLEY

68 Georgian houses, 1–4 Gloucester Place at the corner of North Road, *c.* 1890. They were demolished in 1934 and replaced by Telephone House.

69 (*opposite*) London Road as a residential area: 13, 14 and 15 London Road, three of a terrace of five, 1900. When this now busy road was built in the 1820's and 1830's it consisted mainly of private houses, some quite substantial. The gardens were removed in 1903 when the roadway was widened and the conversion to shops was accelerated

70 The Old Steine, looking north from Royal York Hotel, 1855. This is the oldest existing photograph of the Steine, which at this period was almost entirely residential, being especially favoured by the medical profession. The Victoria Fountain, designed by A. H. Wilds, was inaugurated in May 1846. Behind it was Chantrey's statue of George IV, moved to its present site in Church Street in 1922

71 The Old Steine crossing into Marine Parade, about 1870. The Aquarium had yet to be built; at the right was the Esplanade leading to the Chain Pier, 300 yards distant. Marine Parade, then quite narrow at this point, was widened out over arches when the Aquarium was built in 1872

72 Not many Brightonians will remember this shop at the corner of Peel Place and York Road (now York Hill). Built in the 1850's, these houses adjoined Railway property. In 1905, together with neighbouring Peel Street and Queen Street, they were swept away to provide space for extensions to the Railway Goods Yard

73 Pavilion Parade from Old Steine, *c.* 1868. The houses hidden by trees (right) were Nos. 1 and 2 Old Steine, two of the 'Blues and Buffs' built about 1780 and removed in 1928 for a road-widening which later claimed the houses in Pavilion Parade as far as Pavilion Street (centre)

74 Preston Village looking north, *c.* 1890. On the left, South Road and at the right the high wall of Preston Manor gardens

75 Preston Circus and Viaduct Road; laying the tram rails, 1901. To allow an easy curve into Beaconsfield Road most of Longhurst's Brewery was demolished earlier in this year. The other rails were to take the trams across the Circus into New England Road. The old Hare and Hounds Inn, seen here, was rebuilt in 1905

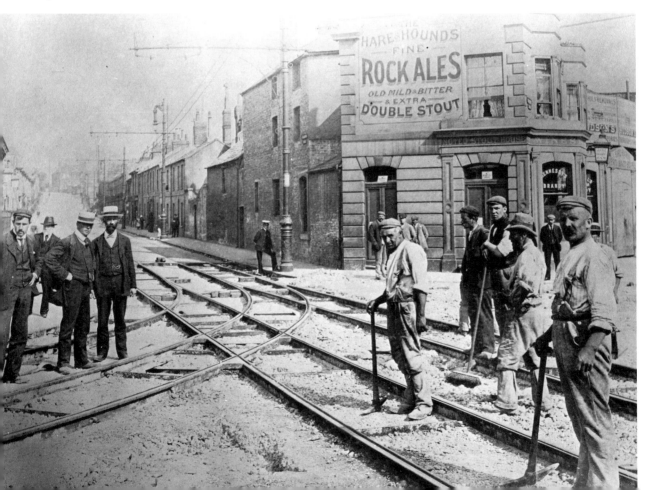

76 Preston Road, 25 August 1909. The solid-tyred Motor Mail Van, travelling south, collided with a lamp standard at the corner of Springfield Road. The motor service had replaced the horse-drawn Parcels van in June 1905. The houses behind the trees have since given way to a large garage and motor showrooms

77 Preston Road; schoolchildren in procession to Preston Park, 9 July 1902. This was in celebration of the Coronation of Edward VII. Owing to the King's illness the Coronation was postponed until 9 August, but the organisers decided that the planned programme should be carried through on the original date

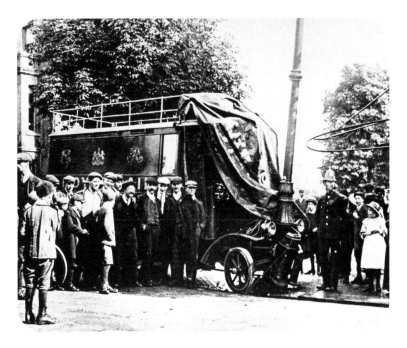

78 (*overleaf*) Brighton College of Art, Grand Parade. Women students in the life class in Edwardian days

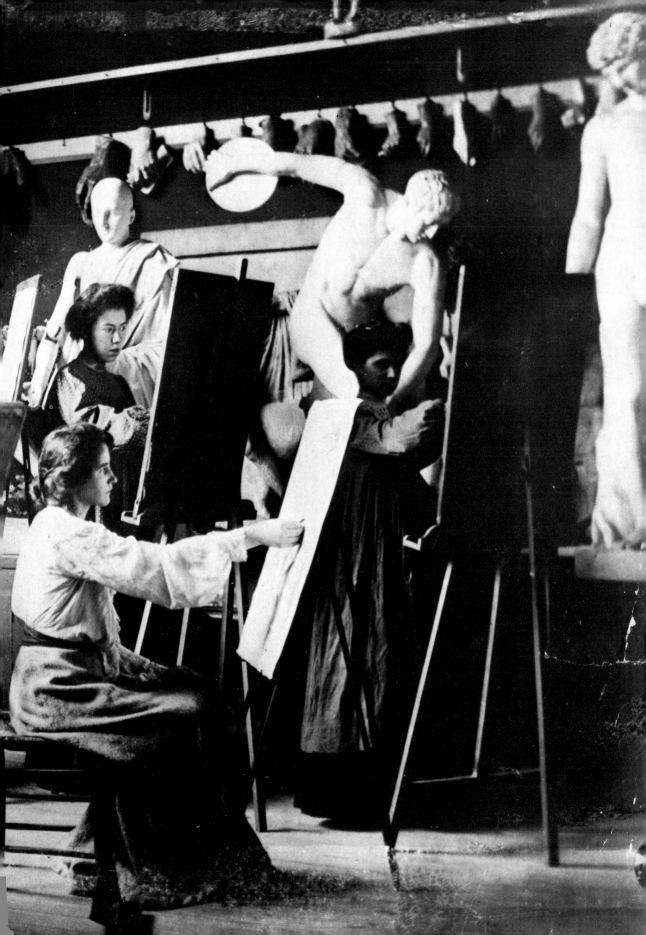

79 London Road, Withdean, during the severe snowstorm of January 1881, said to have been the worst for 50 years. The coal delivery cart is standing a few yards south of the present Tongdean Lane. The barn beyond was removed as recently as 1960 and was replaced by flats

WEST AND NORTH-WEST

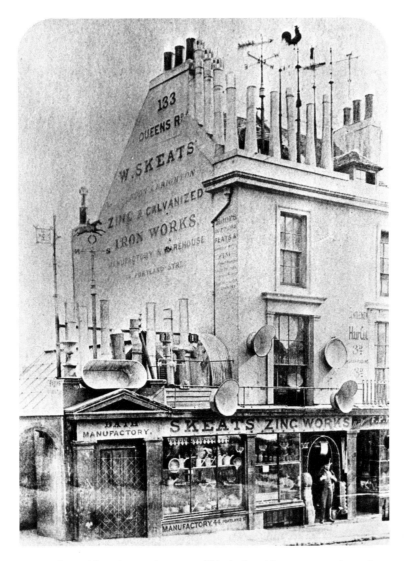

80 A shop with an impressive array of hip baths, chimney pots and weather-vanes, in 1872. W. Skeats of 133 Queens Road was described as Zinc Worker and Bathmaker. The rent of this building was £35 a year. At the barber's shop next door a haircut cost 3d. The entrance to the Regent Cinema, opened in 1921, now covers this site

81 Building the North Road chimney, 1891. The first electricity generating station owned by Brighton Corporation was set up in North Road and led to the erection of the chimney. After the opening of Southwick Power Station in 1906 generating gradually ceased here and the chimney was demolished in 1929

82 Looking down Queens Road from Brighton Station, in 1903. Public transport from the Station was then confined to horse buses and cabs as the Tramway down Queens Road to Old Steine came into operation only in July 1904. The buildings are little changed to-day

83 One of the many shoeing forges in Brighton in late Victorian days: Knight's forge in Regency Mews, about 1890. The premises extended through into what was then 25 Castle Street, where the forge continued until the 1920's

84 Road works in North Road before the rails for the Tramway from Old Steine to Brighton Station were laid in 1904. The houses behind the workmen, although facing into North Road, were Nos. 40 and 41 Marlborough Place. Together with the adjoining Georgian houses they were removed in 1934 for the building of Telephone House

EAST AND NORTH-EAST

85 By the pond of Moulsecoomb Home Farm, 1889. The farm buildings hid
from view the Brighton-Lewes railway embankment which separated Home
Farm from Moulsecoomb Place. Neither the pond nor the buildings remain,
but Woodside School is only a few yards from this spot

86 Lewes Road in 1869, looking towards the unfinished railway viaduct. This viaduct was for the Brighton to Kemp Town line (started in 1866 and opened on 2 August 1869). Through the central archway can be seen the tower of the lodge of the Extra-Mural Cemetery, while the cottages beyond the Viaduct (right) were in Melbourne Street, formerly California Cottages

87 Looking south in Lewes Road in 1901 when the tram rails were being laid. The scene is just north of St Pauls Street when the long line of tall trees still flanked Gladstone Terrace. The trams ran from 25 November 1901 until 1 September 1939

88 (*opposite above*) Crowds on the Race Course for one of the Easter Volunteer Reviews. The exact year is not known but it could have been 1861 or a little later as these Reviews were held for several years. Brighton was then full of Volunteers from Good Friday until Easter Monday, on which day the actual Review took place

89 (*opposite below*) Queens Park on opening day, 10 August 1892. Previously a private estate, the park was bought by Brighton Race Stand Trustees from the trustees of George Duddell and presented to the town, the opening ceremony being performed by the Mayor, Alderman Ewart, M.D.

90 Brighton College Masters, 1871. Included in the group is George Long (1800–1879), second from left in front row. He had been the first Professor of Ancient Languages at the University of Virginia

91   Brighton College: the playing field in 1876, with farm buildings on the hill to the east. College Terrace and Canning Street had yet to be built but, at the extreme left, are the backs of houses on the south side of Hendon Street

92   Brighton College: the Dining Hall, *c.* 1896

HOVE

93 King Edward VII walking on Kingsway, approaching the private gardens. The King made several visits to Hove during the years 1908, 1909, and 1910, often staying with Arthur Sassoon at No. 8 Kings Gardens

94 The full length of Brunswick Terrace, about 1880, showing (extreme right) Western House, Kings Road, built in the 1830's and removed in 1930. At the boundary between Brighton and Hove was the toll-house (left) where duties were levied on all coals brought into Brighton. This duty was introduced in the Brighton Town Act of 1773 and abolished in 1887. The money raised was used for the erection of groynes along the beach

95 The Well House, St Anns Well Gardens, 1891. Formerly part of Wick Farm the Gardens were acquired by Hove Corporation and opened to the public in May 1908. The Well House, which enclosed the chalybeate spring, was demolished in 1937

96 Hove in 1869. Taken from a house in St Aubyns, the picture shows George Street School, St Andrews Church and the Gas Works. The Works were built in 1835 for the Brighton and Hove General Gas Company and gas was produced here until 1870, when the Portslade Works opened. Between the chimney and the Church is the distant Cliftonville (now Hove) Station, opened on 1 October 1865 and then separated from the George Street area by fields

97 The Tithe Barn and other farm buildings in Church Road, May 1892. On the right is the Connaught Hotel in Hove Street. About 1896 Harvey Lewer started to build shops and dwellings along this frontage, which was called Lewer's Terrace (now part of Church Road). Hove Public Library was opened in July 1908, a few yards to the east of the site of the barn

98 (*opposite above*) The Triumphal Arch erected at the Brighton-Hove boundary in Western Road to mark the visit of Edward, Prince of Wales and Princess Alexandra, on 21 July 1881. The structure, less solid than it seemed, was made of wood and canvas suitably coloured and decorated

99 (*opposite below*) How milk was delivered in 1910. Hand carts and horse floats in Western Road, Hove, with a view up Farm Road

100 The band playing on the Brunswick Lawns, 1908. In the background are Adelaide Crescent and the then private gardens

101 Fashionables attending, by invitation, the garden party of the Mayor of Hove, ·Alderman Bruce Morison, June 1906. The party was held on the private lawns of the West Brighton Estate Company facing the Avenues. These lawns were then completely enclosed and the general public normally had no access to them

102 A balloon in the grounds of Brooker Hall, New Church Road, *c.* 1905

103 Schoolchildren in Hove Park on Empire Day, 1907. The houses on the skyline are in Dyke Road, then separated from the park by farmlands. The long wooden fence was removed during the 1930's

104 (*opposite above*) Boys with an oxen-drawn farm cart on the old narrow road between West Blatchington and Hangleton, 2 September 1892

105 (*opposite below*) A circus procession going north in Sackville Road, 16 August 1893, passing on the left, Clarendon Villas, with the entrance to Portland Road behind the leading elephants. The houses in the background are in the Westbourne district

106   The recovery of the Goldstone. This stone stood for many years on farm land at Goldstone Bottom until about 1834 when Farmer Rigden, annoyed by repeated visits to his land by archaeologists, had it buried. At the end of the last century local agitation led to a search and it was brought to light on 29 September 1900. Since 1906 it has been in Hove Park

ROTTINGDEAN

107   Rottingdean Pier, with passengers boarding the sea-going car bound for the Banjo Groyne, Brighton, c. 1900. The steel pier was about 100 yards long; underneath was the plant for generating the electric motive power of the Tramroad

108 (*opposite above*) North End House, Rottingdean, taken while Sir Edward Burne-Jones lived here (1880 until 1898). The house had earlier consisted of two separate cottages, Prospect House and Aubrey Cottage

109 (*opposite below*) Rottingdean from the east in 1896. It was then an old village remote from Brighton, though linked with it by an occasional horse-bus and the Seashore Electric Tramroad

110 (*above*) Looking north along Cliff Terrace in 1890. The horse bus, standing outside the White Horse Hotel, was about to start the journey to Brighton which it made twice a day. Formerly called the King of Prussia, the Hotel was demolished in 1934 and replaced by the present building

111 A group at the wedding of Stanley Baldwin (later Earl Baldwin) and Lucy Ridsdale, photographed on the lawn of The Dene, the home of the bride's father, Edward Lucas Jenks Ridsdale (12 September 1892)

CHURCHES

112 The old mother-church of St Nicholas as it was before the restoration and alterations by Richard Cromwell-Carpenter in 1852–1853. An outside flight of steps gave access to galleries, while the building behind the two boys was a separate chantry. (From a daguerreotype by George Ruff senior, taken about 1850 or possibly even earlier)

113 St Peter's Church, *c.* 1890. Designed by Sir Charles Barry and consecrated on 25 January 1828, it became the Parish Church in 1873. The three-sided apsidal chancel was replaced by the present chancel, by Somers Clarke, in 1906

114 The Countess of Huntingdon's Chapel, North Street, in 1869. This chapel was built in 1774, on the site of a smaller chapel, but had later undergone many alterations and enlargements. Famed for the ministries of Rev Joseph Sortain from 1832 to 1860 and Rev J. B. Figgis from 1861, it was demolished for rebuilding early in 1870

115 St Margaret's Place and St Margaret's Church, *c.* 1879, after the restoration. The church was built, by Cooper and Lynn of Brighton, as a financial speculation by Barnard Gregory and was opened on 26 December 1824. The last service was held on 30 September 1956 and the church was demolished in 1959

116 St Michael's and All Angels, Victoria Road, in its original form by G. E. Bodley. It was opened in 1862 but before long enlargement was needed and a new church was built on vacant land to the north. The new church was designed by William Burges and opened in 1895

WINDMILLS

117 Ballards Mill, Patcham, built in 1791 and removed in 1902. A squat
smock mill, it stood on the ridge to the east of Old London Road not far from the
present Old Mill Close

118 (*opposite above*) West Blatchington Mill, *c*. 1880. A wooden smock-and-bonnet mill, it was built on a square tower from three sides of which radiated large barns. In 1938 Hove Corporation acquired the mill and Holmes Avenue was laid out on either side of it

119 (*below left*) Tower Mill, Ditchling Road, *c*. 1893. This was built in 1838 and had four floors, a cap and an outer roundhouse with the roof used as deck. Its last owners were C. Cutress & Son, whose shop in Round Hill Road adjoined the mill. It was demolished in 1913 and the red brick houses of Belton Road now cover the site

120 (*below right*) Windmill at Lewes Prison, *c*. 1875. First erected in 1802 at Pipes Passage, St Michaels, Lewes it was moved a few years later to the Prison site. The mill was heightened by 20 feet in 1853. The sweeps and fan were removed in 1912 and the mill itself was demolished in 1922

121 (*above*) Hodsons Black Mill, photographed by Edward Fox on the day of its demolition, 25 June 1866. This was a 12-sided smock mill which stood in West Hill Road and was built in 1804. The brick base remained for another century. It was used as a store and garage, and was removed only a few years ago

122 (*overleaf*) Clayton Mills (Jack and Jill) *c*. 1910. 'Jack', a tower mill with a domed revolving top, was built in 1876 and still survives minus its sails. 'Jill', formerly Lashmar's mill, stood in Dyke Road near Belmont until about 1848 when it was removed to above Clayton, drawn up the hill by oxen

SPORT

123   C. B. Fry (Sussex) and Major Poore (Hampshire) at the County Ground, Hove (believed to have been on 4 August 1904.) The houses of Cromwell Road are in the background

124   (*opposite above*) Playing croquet on the old Lewes Bowling Green in Castle Precincts, *c.* 1870. This bowling green dates from the seventeenth century and the wooden pavilion still stands

125   (*opposite below*) Members of Roedean School Archery Club in the garden at Sussex Square, in 1890. The cental figure is Miss Millicent Lawrence, one of the Founders of the school

BRIGHTON & HOVE ALBION F.C.
1909-10

A. NELMES   G. WHITING   J. ROBSON   W. CRINSON   J. BUTT.
J. McGHIE. G. WHITTINGTON. J. LUMLEY. R. ROUTLEDGE. F. BLACKMAN H. MIDDLETON. W. BOOTH. E.H. ELLIOTT
A. ARMSTRONG. G. FEATHERSTONE W. CONNOR. A.E. LONGSTAFFE J. LEEMING. C.G. WEBB. W.H. JONES. W. HASTINGS. H. LONGSTAFFE
J.H. EACOCK.   J. COLMAN.   R. CRAIG.   J. HAWORTH

126   Brighton and Hove Albion Football Club, 1909–1910. The players are grouped in front of the small West Stand (removed as recently as 1958). This team won the Southern League, the Southern Charity Cup, and the Football Association Charity Shield, beating Aston Villa, Division I champions, at Stamford Bridge by 1–0

127   The Sussex County Cricket Team of 1864 photographed on the Royal Brunswick Ground, showing part of the thatched pavilion. This ground, which was where the Avenues are today, was opened on 26 May 1848, and was replaced by the present County Ground in 1872

128   Motor Speed Trials, July 1905. The cars are standing at the top of the slope leading down to Madeira Drive just above where Black Rock swimming pool is today. The house to the left is No. 1 Madeira Terrace, removed in 1932

129   Cycling. A meeting of cyclists in Old Steine, *c*. 1877

130 Swimming. The Men's bathing beach just east of the skeleton of the Palace Pier, *c.* 1895. Free bathing was then permitted only from certain designated public bathing places before 8 a.m. and after 8 p.m.

TRANSPORT

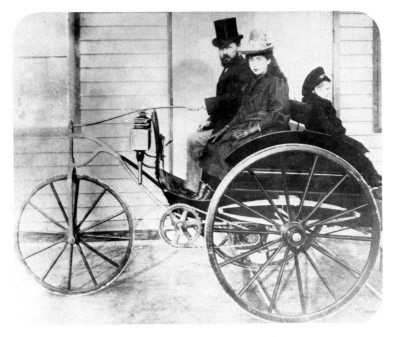

131   Magnus Volk in his electric dog-cart in Madeira Drive, 1887

132 A four-in-hand outside Moulsecoomb Place, *c.* 1899. The gentleman holding the reins was Mr B. Rogers-Tillstone, the owner of Moulsecoomb Place

133 (*opposite above*) A trip to the Devil's Dyke in 1895. The wagonette is taking on passengers from its start in Kings Road at the foot of West Street. As horse traffic declined the protective kerbside iron railings became an unnecessary obstruction. They were removed in stages, the last going in 1926

134 (*opposite below*) The three-horse bus which plied between the Royal Oak Hotel, Rottingdean and Brighton Station. The journey took about an hour. The scene is near the present busy Rottingdean cross-roads, now controlled by traffic lights

135 (*opposite*) The long line of horse cabs in Terminus Road adjoining Brighton Station, in 1903. These were the unlicensed cabs which had to form a queue, only two cabs being allowed in the Station forecourt at any one time. Licensed cabs stood inside the Station

136 (*above*) Cars arriving at the Hotel Metropole on Saturday, 14 November 1896. This was on the occasion of the inaugural 'procession' of cars from London to Brighton which followed the passing of the Act removing restrictions on motor cars used on public roads

137 A unique conception of Magnus Volk, originator of the earlier Volk's Electric Railway, 'Daddy Long-legs', as it was affectionately called, had only a short life, from 29 November 1896 to 1901. 'Daddy Long-legs' travelling east between Black Rock and Rottingdean, *c*. 1900. This low-tide picture shows the double rails, standards and overhead wires. Though all these have long since gone, the concrete blocks on which the rails were laid can still be seen 70 years later

138 The sea-going car—the interior. In the centre was an upholstered knifeboard type seat with other seats at the far end. Plants and flowers occupied the space between the seat backs. Many of the windows, particularly on the seaward side were heavily curtained

139 The sea-going car of the Brighton and Rottingdean Seashore Electric Tramroad nearing the landing platform at Banjo Groyne, 1898

140 Tramcars 7 and 25 standing at the terminal loops at the Pavilion with Marlborough Place beyond, *c.* 1902. The extension to the Old Steine was opened in July 1904 and this then remained the terminus until the trams finished running in September 1939

141 Crowds leaving the Race Course and boarding waiting tramcars at the top of Elm Grove, in the 1900's. At the right is the flint wall of the Workhouse, built in 1866; it is now Brighton General Hospital

LONDON BRIGHTON
AND SOUTH COAST RAILWAY

142 Craven locomotive 2-4-0 No. 12, photographed at Lovers Walk, May
1858. John Chester Craven is seen seated with his family and his personal staff

143 The Chalk Hill, from Prestonville Road, *c.* 1859. When the Brighton to Shoreham Railway was constructed in 1839 the line was driven through the solid chalk of the West Hill. To the north-east of the cutting this chalk hill remained and took many years to remove. The bridge carrying New England Road over the railway is little changed to this day

144 A panoramic view of the Preston area, between the Railway and Ditchling Road, about 1860. Taken from the Chalk Hill above New England and Old Shoreham Roads (on either side of the trees) the photograph shows market gardens and farm lands on both sides of the Viaduct. A few buildings can be seen in Ditchling Road, on the far right

145 A train for Brighton at the Dyke Railway Station, *c.* 1905. The old carriage on the platform was used as refreshment rooms. The Dyke Railway, which opened on 1 September 1887, closed on 31 December 1938, and the station is now part of a farm

146 The locomotive running sheds on a Sunday in October 1903, showing engines at rest. More than 40 engines are coaled-up. Many had brought down week-end excursionists

147 Shoreham-by-sea Station, 1870, showing the low platforms and early forms of signalling

148 Excursion locomotives in Brighton Station on a Bank Holiday, about 1904, awaiting the signal to enter the locomotive yard. At the head of this coupled line was the 'D2 Class' locomotive 309 (withdrawn in 1906). Note the 'Double Diamond' headcode (Specials) on the engines

ROUND AND ABOUT

149 Shoreham Harbour, with a stern view of the barque *Libanonaland*; 2 October 1890

150 Shoreham Harbour. The barque *Siiwo Abo* and paddle boat *Mistletoe* at Southwick on 10 May 1890. In the background, Courtney and Birkett's boat yard and the houses in Albion Street

151 Portslade Gas Works and the Canal, *c*. 1870. The workmen are waiting on the gantry for the wherry to transport them across the canal, thus avoiding a long walk around via Aldrington

152 Devils Dyke—the cleft and Suspension Railway. This bridge was opened on 13 October 1894, and was operated by the Telpher Cable and Cliff Railway Syndicate Ltd. The distance between the two columns was 650 feet, while the complete span from one end to the other was 1200 feet. The car carried eight passengers, the fare being 6d for the two-minute journey

153 The Dyke Steep Grade Railway, as seen from near Poynings, about 1903. One car descended as the other ascended. Opened on 24 July 1897, with a fare of 2d each way, it operated for several years, but ceased working about 1908

154 Lancing College and Chapel, from the east, 1884. The apse was built up first because Nathaniel Woodard, the founder, feared that after his death his successors might not have the courage to build the Chapel up to its full height